I0846383

NAPOLEON

WAY OF THE CONQUEROR

7 LEADERSHIP LESSONS HE USED & ABUSED

BY

MARK WEEKS

Books by Mark Weeks

Code of the Conqueror – The Journey

Soul of a Dream Catcher

Conquerors: Military History Quotes 450BC – 1788AD

Mum-Ultrapreneur

Timeless Wisdom: 701 Inspirational Quotes to Conquer Life

Code of the Conqueror - Golden Sayings of Yelu Bao-Zhi

Concise Law of Attraction

Another book published by

azuni.world

'Where passion meets knowledge.'

For my mentors

Kerry Donovan & Robert C Brown

Thank you for revealing the way to

following my bliss.

First Published in Great Britain 2021 by Azuni World ©

Copyright © Mark Weeks All rights reserved 2021

Mark Weeks has asserted his right under the Copyright, Designs and Patents Act 1988 to be identified as the author of

Napoleon – Way of the Conqueror.

No part of this publication may be reproduced, stored in or introduced into a retrieval system, or transmitted, in any form, or by any means (electronic, mechanical, photocopying, recording or otherwise) without the prior written permission of the publisher.

Images within book ©Copyright Imagerie Pellerin – Épinal 1962

Cover Design by 100Covers.com

TABLE OF CONTENTS

INTRODUCTION

'Nurture your mind with great thoughts;

to believe in the heroic makes heroes,'

~ Disraeli,

UK Prime Minister and author.

In Tibetan Buddhism, books always open with short poems. The tradition is, if you understand the poem, there is little need to undertake reading the whole book.

My take on this philosophy is:

If you can relate to the following passage by Friedrich Nietzsche, you must undertake reading the book often, since it will serve you well forever.

'Independence is for the very few; it is a privilege of the strong. And whoever attempts it even with the best right but without inner constraint proves that he is probably not only strong, but also daring to the point of recklessness.

He enters into a labyrinth, he multiplies a
thousand-fold the dangers which life brings
with it in any case, not the least of which is
that no one can see how and where he loses
his way, becomes lonely, and is torn
piecemeal by some minotaur of conscience.

Supposing one like that comes to grief, this
happens so far from the comprehension of
men that they neither feel it nor sympathise.

And he cannot go back any longer.

Nor can he go back to the pity of men,'

~ Friedrich Nietzsche, philosopher and
writer.

Nietzsche, I believe, considered
Emperor Napoleon I such a man. The
Mediterranean adventurer journeyed from
humble beginnings in Corsica to ruling most
of Europe. As a Captain, he broke the siege of
Toulon. As a General, he stormed Egypt, and
as an Emperor, he invaded Spain and Russia,
simultaneously, even though in doing so, it
culminated in a horde of horrors, which
ultimately led to his downfall, and to his
ultimate imprisonment on that 'wretched
rock'.

Upon reflection, Napoleon's downfall

became inevitable, since coalition after coalition set out to destroy both his vision, and his appetite for power and glory. And reflection—where we are all seated today—is where our problems start. Seemingly, we appear wiser and virtuous to those of the past, quick to judge and condemn others—especially those who have the deaths of millions on their hands.

We will never truly understand history or the inner minds of those who rose to great heights unless we immerse ourselves in their lives and try our utmost to understand the world they inhabited without pre-conceived judgement, self-righteousness or condemnation. Is it possible to look at the life of Napoleon in this context?

In the words of Napoleon, 'To understand the man, you have to know what was happening in the world when he was twenty.'

If we take this approach to history, we might generate a better understanding of our ancestors and the paths they forged. And possibly, we may even begin to appreciate that for Napoleon's daring to the point of recklessness, he had unwittingly multiplied his dangers a thousand-fold, until he became lost and wasted his God given talents. The path he chose to tread was so far removed from the comprehension of the average man at the beginning of the 19th Century, that, after his defeat he could no longer go back to their pity since no one truly understood or sympathised with him. Let's see whether we can do him greater justice two hundred years after his demise.

In earlier times, Napoleon always gave credit to his lucky star, feeling as though he could do no wrong—as did so many of his benefactors. At the time, he was a tour de force, incomparable to another. Napoleon's desire for greatness was stimulated by his extensive reading, where he learned about the great feats of rulers such as Frederick the Great, Alexander the Great, Charlemagne, and Julius Caesar. A continual thirst for knowledge made Napoleon the master and commander of the majority of Europe.

Untypically, I have undertaken this work in the first person and have used the basis of Napoleon dictating notes to General Bertrand whilst imprisoned on St. Helena. The series of notes were created for the sole purpose of guiding his 'official' son, Napoleon II, The King of Rome, in his quest to be future leader of his people. A quest, which did not come to fruition, since Napoleon II sadly died from consumption at the age of twenty-one.

Although a work of fiction, the following passages reveal the leadership and interpersonal skills with which Napoleon I was naturally gifted, and which led him to greatness, plus his many regrets. For the purpose of flow, I have used a narrative style and a certain creative license. I hope my efforts to duplicate the tone of Napoleon has had no deleterious effect upon his ethos and are added purely to clarify and enhance the conversational style I have adopted. The reference works which have helped me write this book are shown within the bibliography, along with added historical notes and a chronology of events.

The seven essential lessons used are based upon my own **SPARKLE** Principle, created to help trim our desires and aid our own self-mastery. The **SPARKLE** Principle forms part of my Code of the Conqueror – Art of Manfulness framework. All of which, fits rather conveniently into Napoleon's fascination with his own lucky star.

Mark Weeks.
May 2021

1819

LETTER TO
NAPOLEON II
THE KING OF ROME

20th March 1819

Napoleon II,

If all has gone to plan, you will receive this letter on your 16th birthday, along with four hundred volumes, selected from those in my library of which I have been accustomed to use the most. I fear, I will have died long before you receive this.

Today, my son, you are a man. Yet on such a grandiose occasion, the only thing I may truly offer you is the counsel that follows.

Please do not dismiss these missives as the ramblings of an old man, for within these short notes lies the keys to the governance of men and to your future prosperity.

From the outset, I urge you to remember that men tend not to learn very much from the lessons of history, which is perhaps, the most important of all the lessons of history. You, my son, must be different.

I will preach no further ... it is up to you to follow your own star of destiny. As a father, all I can do is prepare you for your own experiences.

My darling son, to not see you grow and become a man is the greatest defeat I have ever known. Of all my privations, the most painful, the one I shall never get used to, is being parted from you and your mother. It is one I would never wish upon my greatest adversaries. Yet this is my fate, as I know I will never see you again. Cast away on this wretched rock in the middle of the Atlantic, I feel my health deteriorating and strength ebbing away. And though surrounded with gallant disciples, I find my energy and enthusiasm for their daily discourses boring, and their tittle-tattle tiresome. My single comfort is having a marble bust of yourself on my bedroom mantlepiece.

My days are now filled with recounting

and dictating my epic rise to power and re-living 'what if' tactics with the faithful de Montholon and Bertrand. In fact, it was Bertrand who suggested I prepare these notes and whose memory for such detail has aroused me from my slumber and helped ease the pain of being so far from you. For we must be employed, as occupation is the scythe of time. After all, a man ought to fulfil his destinies. This is my grand doctrine, and one I feel compelled to accomplish.

I have set forth this series of transcripts for your personal attention only. They are not to be read once and forgotten. Study them well over the course of time and let them resonate within your being.

Great ambition is the passion of a great character. Those endowed with it may perform very good or very bad acts. It all depends on the principles which direct them. The principles discussed within these epistles represent the lives of every living man, yet many ignore such facts and are manipulated, led and used by those who have mastered them.

Within these words you will find the secrets of my successes. You will also find greater detail in my failings. As I am well aware, in life, people always ask after one's victories, yet no one is so eager to learn how one has failed.

You have much to study. Much is expected of you. You will not learn to conquer the hearts of men by listening to your Grandfather, for Francis is not a true leader. He did not rise through the ranks, nor was he uplifted by the soul of a nation. He was merely born into royalty and wealth. Much the same will be said of you, I fear.

Yet, you are different. You have the blood of Emperor Napoleon running through your veins! You have no choice but to be the best you can. Expect adversity. For some, playing with your emotions is purely a game, and they will relish every opportunity to defeat you. This is guaranteed. Only by fortitude and enduring such ridicule will you develop the skills required to rise above a system that wishes to see the end of our bloodline.

I therefore enclose my wisdom, love and admiration. Now, stand strong in the storm, master yourself and reach far into the future. Eclipse your father, yet never forget his glorious past. Then ... then, as your father, I will dare whisper, I have not lived in vain.

Emperor Napoleon I,
Longwood,
St Helena

SELF-MASTERY

'The first and greatest victory is to
conquer yourself.
To be conquered by yourself
is of all things most shameful and vile,'
~ Plato.

It is my belief there is no distinction between fatherhood and true leadership, they are both one and the same. I would choose to love and command one man by the same principles as I would the 100,000 men who march behind me. From this point, I will refer to you *not* as my own flesh and blood, but as a young commander, ready to take to the field of battle—that is, the battle of life.

An inscription at the Oracle of Delphi

in Greece reads, 'Know Thyself'. This is the starting point in the governance of men. To live is to suffer, and a human being who is worthy of honour must always struggle for mastery of self. Therefore, the most powerful skill of all is the ability to reflect honestly on one's own abilities. How can you conquer the hearts of men if you cannot control your own? Your strengths, your weaknesses, must be at your command. They must be under your guard. No one with the audacity to test your strength can be aware of your weaknesses. Therefore, your guiding principle is that you must look into yourself before you can look out into the world.

Great events hang by a thread. The able man turns everything to profit and neglects nothing that may give him one chance more. The man of lesser ability, by overlooking just one thing, spoils the whole. And, for me, every time I had one chance, I multiplied it again and again. Maybe it was no coincidence that I had an uncommon appreciation for calculations from such an early age. I would study mathematics relentlessly, even before the age of nine. My father added a little room to the side of our home for me to study alone, which I did every day. Numbers became my first ally. And, to this day, I firmly believe that to be a good General, a man must know mathematics, for it is of daily help in straightening one's ideas. As a child, I took great pride in showing off my work to my mother and father in front of my siblings, especially Joseph. Though these idyllic times were not to last, my father's connections and our noble status gave rise to the opportunity for schooling in France.

At the age of nine, I left my beloved Corsica with a heavy heart. As the oldest son, Joseph was to become a priest, and I, an army cadet. On the journey to the mainland, I recall my father reassuring us that ability without opportunity is worthless. And this was to be the greatest opportunity he would ever give us. After a short and intensive introduction into the French language, Joseph and I separated. His tears stung the side of my face, while I remained stoic, hiding my emotions, which I continued to do for the next seven years.

By the time I become a Lieutenant in 1791, I knew the feelings of my heart, and I knew men. I was not made like any of those I had seen. I venture to believe that I am not made like any of those who are in existence. If I am not better, I am at least different, and this I will believe to my dying day. If you are to be a leader of men, you too, will need an inborn belief in your own abilities. This belief can never falter, which is why I must repeat once more, look into yourself before you can look out into the world. There is no other way.

Did you hear I worked the whole time? It is true. A genie did not suddenly reveal to me that which I must say or do in any given circumstance. No. It was my reflection, my meditation.

The hours I spent in a hot bath or in front of the fire were not idle but were always productive. During such times, I had the daily news read to me, and I listened to my own inner voice. This inner voice especially, would be my guiding star.

My young commander, as you learn the art of self-study, you must learn to question everything you read and hear, and you must always consider the source. Try your best to remain sceptical rather than negative. For far too many years I listened intently on advice from Talleyrand. From the death of the Duke d'Enghien to the attempted conquests of Spain and Russia, all of it started from that piece of shit in silk stockings. At least I had the foresight to have spies placed upon my 'chief of spies' Fouche, for all the good it did. He, no doubt, set his own spies upon my spies. What a tangled web we wove.

As a leader you must remain calm. All eyes will be forever on you, even those times when you think you are alone. Things go wrong, often terribly wrong. Keep calm whilst everyone around you panics. Imagine looking down upon yourself, as if viewing a game of chess. This detachment will serve you well. Although I was seen to lose my temper on several occasions to good effect, these episodes were merely theatrics—all of them. From the smashing of valuable china, to outbursts aimed at Talleyrand in front of others, mere theatrics. Underneath, though, I maintained control. And you must do the same, my young commander. Keep control.

Uncontrolled passion and anger give a skewed perception of reality and you must remain vigilant. I feel you will be asking, why didn't I control myself with the treacherous English—*La Perfide Albion?* Well, surrounded by that bloody moat and dwelling in their ivory towers, their financing of coalitions against my Empire and the constant taunting with their condescending attitude, what choice did I have? I was young, and after all, am I not a Corsican at heart?

After the collapse of peace in 1803, I had had more than enough of their sneering and their deception. I reorganized our navy and created the Army of England. The English wanted us to jump the ditch and so we would. We went to war earlier than I had planned. With my usual vigour, I set forth plans to be in London within five days. However, by that time, the gales of December arrived, and with the English frigates continuing to prowl close to our shores like hungry sharks, the moment had gone. Although I was prepared to lose 20,000 men on crossing, I knew once more that the nation of shopkeepers was safe for a while longer. Yet they always feared me.

Ah, Pitt, he told them truly, 'There is no safety for you with a man who carries a whole invasion in his head'. Maybe he was right. But look at me now, I am gorged with glory, I turned it into litter. It takes time and effort to know your true self. This is why so few do. And even fewer are fit enough to lead men. Such self-reflection requires discipline and persistence. I would spend hour upon hour reading and studying whilst my fellow officers did naught but womanise and debauch of themselves. My worthy habits are always overlooked when they, the historians, examine my rise to power. They put my success down to Barras, Saliceti or even my incomparable Josephine and her murky past. Of course, a little luck plays its part, but preparation holds the key, and when the opportunities of life present themselves, clasp them with both hands and never let go.

I will finish today by adding that there are but two powers in the world: the power of the sword and the power of the mind. In the long run, the sword is always beaten by the mind. But when married together, what bliss.

POWER

Everyone admires the bold; no one honours the timid.

A man must have accomplished all that I have, before he is able to realize fully the difficulty of doing good. Sometimes, it needed all my power to succeed. I had raised myself from nothing to become the most powerful monarch in the world and therefore, from experience, I have one prime counsel for you—be master. For it is better to be the one who eats rather than the one who is eaten. For me, in times gone by, the revolution was the mistress of the hour. One could not struggle against it. One had to accommodate oneself to the task.

But how will you start?

In the words of Epictetus, the Greek

Stoic philosopher, 'Make the best use of what is in your power and take the rest as it happens.' And, when the rest starts to happen, there is no greater feeling in the world. It is more intoxicating than a beautiful woman, for with power, no woman is out of reach. Women? Maybe a lesson for another day, my young commander. Until now, I would go so far to say that power was my mistress. I had done too much to conquer her to let her be snatched from me. Although, it seemed that power dropped into my hands in the most natural way. Some might even say that power arrived on its own accord. Yet I know what labour, what sleepless nights, what scheming was involved in the process of acquiring her.

True power starts by imposing yourself on the public imagination. Everyone who has succeeded in leading men can verify the fact that it takes persistent effort to impose one's will upon one's people. Much learning from mistakes must be made—of which my early days revisiting Corsica can attest.

Yes, as you have gathered, I loved power, but it was as an artist that I loved it. I loved it as a musician loves his violin, to draw out its sounds and chords and harmonies. But look at me now, how I have fallen. I, whose activity knew no bounds, whose mind never slumbered. I am plunged into a stupor, in a lethargy and have to make an effort to raise my eyelids. And yet what a pleasant thing is rest. My bed has become a place of happiness for me. I would not exchange it for all the thrones of the universe.

How can one fall in such a way and lose such power? Is it by himself, by the hand of providence or by disloyal subjects who never knew they were to be disloyal until tested? It is by all three, completed in rapid succession, and without reprieve.

A great reputation is built on self-confidence and in creating a great noise, the more there is made, the farther off it is heard. Laws, institutions, monuments, nations, may all fall, but the noise continues, and it resounds for ages. To have such power and control breeds only more power and more control. But, let it be said, winning is not enough if one fails to take advantage of the success. **Exaggeration is key.**

In war everything is mental. Man is naturally inclined to believe in the absolute and inevitable rule of numbers, and greater numbers will always defeat lesser numbers. I once berated my brother, Joseph, for being foolish enough to reveal the actual strength of his armies in Spain. I had it conveyed to him that when induced to reveal the strength of his forces, he should exaggerate by doubling or trebling the number. And by the same token, whenever he mentioned the enemy, he should diminish their forces by half or one third. The same holds true on reporting bulletins. In fact, I had acquired, quite naturally, a predisposition to make bad news seem better, fair news sound good, and exceptional news sound like the most dazzling revelations known to man.

I always knew that I must dazzle and astonish. I also knew that were I to give absolute liberty to the press, my power would not last three days. So, one must control those with eager tongues and pens with an iron fist. Forget the velvet glove, as four hostile newspapers are to be feared far more than a thousand bayonets.

It is true. A leader is purely a dealer in hope, and I had hoped with all my heart. But what would I have changed? Nothing.

With my supreme self-confidence and preparation, nothing could be beyond my reach. God had given me the will and the force to overcome all obstacles. To complete my career, only adversity was wanting, and adversity came. But I digress and talk of years as they were days. Truth be told, days on this wretched rock seem to last years.

'If you have no confidence in self, you are twice defeated in the race of life. With confidence you have won before you have started,' ~ Cicero.

When I read these words from Cicero in my youth, I started to understand the need to believe in oneself more than in others. My confidence soared even higher after the Battle of Lodi. In those days, I knew no fear. There was not a bullet made that would stop me. Even today my heart beats a little faster as I recall seeing the world flee before me. It is as though I were being carried in the air. In the evening of Lodi, I believed myself to be a superior man. Only then did the ambition come to me of executing the great things which, until this point, had been occupying my thoughts only as a fantastic dream. It was then the idea came to me that I could well become, after all, a decisive actor on the political scene. It was then that the first sparks of high ambition were born. A few days after the Battle of Lodi was the first time that I had not complied with the *Directoire's* orders.

After Lodi, nothing would ever be the same again.

If my future had laid purely as a military commander, my power would have dissipated, my victories would have simply faded into the lessons delivered at military schools. But, like Julius Caesar and Frederick the Great, my political genius sets me apart from others. It is through this highest embodiment that statesmen shape the destinies of others. It is this less travelled path where true greatness lies. And, my young commander, for you to possess and manipulate for the better or for the worse, you too must always prioritize capturing the imaginations of others.

For me, the name of king was outworn. It carried with it a trail of obsolete ideas and would make me nothing more than the heir of dead men's glories. I did not wish to be dependent upon a predecessor. The title of Emperor is greater than that of any king. Its significance is not fully explicable, and therefore it stimulates the imagination of the people.

Ah, but what is a throne? A wooden frame covered with velvet. *I am the throne ... France stood more in need of me than I did of Her.* Then again, what is a crown, you may ask? Insignia, I must answer. A statesman must have the insignia of power, for the dull populace cannot believe in the reality of power unless he who wields power wears the insignia. And, with such insignia, I had soldiers and the people on my side. A man who could not rule under such conditions would be an idiot. I did not usurp the crown after all. It was in the gutter and I picked it out with my sword. The people placed it on my head, and I respected their act.

I am the authority. I could influence grown men, more so than I did the Legion of Honour, for it was just a title. Yet men clamour for recognition and praise. Remember, it is not titles that honour men, but men that honour titles. Sometimes, men deserve the contempt which they inspire in me. I have only to put some gold lace on the coat of my virtuous republicans, and they immediately become just what I wish them to be.

The men who have changed the world never succeeded by winning over the powerful, but always by stirring the masses. The first method is a resort to intrigue and only brings limited results. The latter is the course of genius and changes the face of the world. And when finally, power is yours, and yours alone, then the work begins. Everything up to that point is preparation. You must utilise every ounce of strength you can muster and receive every morsel of information regarding your enemies' position, strengths and weaknesses. Then exploit the information with unbridled passion. You must become a master of deception. There is no finer truth than this. And, when you finally have an enemy under your power, deprive him of the means of ever injuring you. Finally, n**ever interrupt him when he is making mistakes.**

Comparable to Machiavelli, I acknowledge that a ruler who can honour his word is generally praised by others. However, history demonstrates time and time again that the ruler achieves the most success when he is crafty, cunning, and better able to trick others. Just look at those who rule England. To quote Machiavelli once more, there are two ways of fighting: by law or by force. Laws come naturally to men, and force comes naturally to beasts. In order to succeed, the ruler must learn how to fight both with laws and with force—he must become half man and half beast. When you use force, you act like a beast. You therefore must learn to act like two types of beasts—lions and foxes. A fox is defenceless against wolves, a lion is defenceless against traps. As a ruler of men, you must learn to act like the fox to recognise traps and like the lion to frighten away the wolves.

Nature gave me a proud and strong character. Had this pride not been in my soul, I could not have risen to the greatest throne of the Universe. And for you? You must always listen and observe, take advantage of every opportunity, for fortune is a woman. If you miss her today, do not expect to find her tomorrow.

I have now become a sort of lay figure, having lost my liberty of action and happiness, and I envy you your lucky fate. At the head of brave men, you will accomplish great things.

And so, my young commander, for you, the battle of life has begun in earnest, and victory will only belong to the most perseverant, since ambition is never content, even on the summit of greatness. And, as Goethe so famously stated, 'Dream no small dreams, for they have no power to move the hearts of men.'

I have the fullest confidence in you and your dreams. For now, it is time for action.

ACTION

'We are what we repeatedly do,'

~ Aristotle.

This evening, Bertrand read aloud several passages from Guibert's General Essay on Tactics. It brought back a flood of youthful memories. Whilst stationed in Valence, I would read these same words over and over. I recall the energy I was storing up at the time, knowing that one day, it would be ready to erupt. All I needed was to keep taking action, for true passion can only be revealed through action.

I feel it is worth noting my favourite passage:

'A man will arise, perhaps from obscurity and the crowd, a man who will not

have made a name for himself, either by speeches or his writings, a man who will have meditated in silence ... This man will seize possession of opinion, circumstance and fortune ...'

I felt I was that man of whom Guibert spoke. I was biding my time for that initial spark to be seen, heard and respected.

As a young officer in 1793, I wanted nothing more than glory. Yet, at the time I was worried for my family. At the time of the siege of Toulon, my mother and siblings were expelled from Corsica and then once more from Toulon. They finally found a refuge of sorts in Marseilles. As for me, I was no closer to finding power. I needed a battlefield to show my true worth. With the mass emigration of royalist officers, trained professionals were worth their weight in gold at the time. I had to be patient for only a little longer before my destiny could be revealed.

At the beginning of the siege of Toulon, I was busy loading gunpowder onto confiscated carts near Nice. How the days dragged. I had to create my own luck, and once more, I set about writing another pamphlet. This time, my work was titled, *Souper de Beaucaire*, which I published at my own expense. I conceived the idea to win favour with Jacobin overlords and to vent my fear of invading continental armies. The pamphlet spoke of siege warfare and included quotations taken from the Chevalier du Teil's treatise on artillery. All I had to do was create fictional characters. So confident was I that I had written a masterpiece, I sent it to nearby Jacobin representatives, one of whom was my Corsican ally, Cristoforo Saliceti. He and his colleague, Gasparin, welcomed the work and had more copies printed and distributed, which was undertaken by Marc Aurel, an old bookshop friend from Valence, who had been appointed 'printer to the revolutionary army'. See how connections add up over such little time? Now this is the power of taking action and believing in oneself.

The momentum and feedback from the representatives encouraged me to write directly to the war minister to request a promotion to lieutenant colonel and a posting to the Army of the Rhine. Unbeknownst to me at the time, the minister asked local dignitaries to validate my loyalty and my ability.

From this one pamphlet—and the years of preparation it represented—Saliceti and Gasparin believed that fate had sent them a miracle. They informed the Committee in Paris of my removal from the Army of Italy and sent me, Captain Buonaparte, to Ollioules as provisional commander of Carteaux's rag tag artillery.

Although I had had several skirmishes to my credit—some of which I have never spoken of—the siege of Toulon was my first opportunity to show my true capacity. That rebellious town was being victualled by British ships. So long as these ships entered the harbour at will, we could not starve the city. It was obvious from the outset what to do. Any cadet who had attended a course in military strategy would have known what to do. The difference was—I did it.

The promontory of Cape L'Eguillette commanded the harbour. I presented my plan, and it was quickly approved. I took the promontory, mounted my cannon there, drove off counterattacks, and then turned my guns on the British ships. They had little choice but to flee. We commanded the harbour, and no more food could reach Toulon. I have always felt the English in general know nothing of the affairs of the Continent, particularly those of France. The city fell and with it the hope of the royalists.

During the siege I never left my men nor batteries, when I needed rest, I slept on the ground wrapped in a cloak.

I become a hero because I saw what any

soldier should have known enough to see. And of course, I acted with vigour and determination. I said to my gunners, 'This is the battery of the men without fear', and they believed me. Thinking themselves without fear, they become so. Ah, the power of the mind, as I have said, war is mental.

Had I fallen face down in the mud at Toulon, my career would have ended before it had truly begun. What cannoneers would have credited me when I told them, 'This is the battery of the men without fear'? Who would have believed in my star of destiny? Who would have followed me on the road to empire?

It takes courage to take action. As to moral courage, I have rarely met with the two o'clock-in-the-morning-kind. I mean unprepared courage, that which is necessary or an unexpected occasion; and which, in spite of the most unforeseen events, leaves full freedom of judgement and decision. I am eminently endowed with this two o'clock-in-the-morning courage, and I have met very few people who are equal in this respect to myself. I recall instructing my secretaries at the Tuileries that during the night they must enter my chambers as seldom as possible. 'Do not awake me when you have any good news to communicate.' I would say, because with such news there is no hurry. 'But when you bring bad news, rouse me instantly.' For then there was not a moment to be lost, immediate action was required!

For me, the grand principle of war is that an army ought always to be ready—by day and by night, and at all hours—to make all the resistance it is capable of making, and targeted at the enemy's weakest point. For, there is a movement in engagements when the least manoeuvre is decisive and gives a victory. It is the single drop of water which makes the vessel overflow.

I have always believed that one must never run away. One must always go forwards and meet one's enemy head on. Yet before such action, you must note, there has never been a man more pusillanimous than I when planning a campaign. I purposely exaggerated all the dangers and all the calamities that circumstances might make possible. I was in a thoroughly painful state of agitation. This did not keep me from looking quite serene in front of my entourage. But once I made up my mind, everything was forgotten except that which led to success. That was the time for action. I just stopped thinking and forged ahead. For we should always go before our enemies with confidence, otherwise our apparent uneasiness inspires them with greater boldness.

Of course, one might say I did not overexaggerate the dangers and calamities of that Spanish ulcer or the invasion of Russia. Granted, I did not foresee the tragedy unrolling before my eyes, but times had changed by 1812, and I still have much to explain to you.

Maybe now would be as a good a time as any to vent my frustrations, as action can lead to destruction within a blink of an eye. And as I told the Polish noblemen on my return to Paris after the Russian debacle, 'from the sublime to the ridiculous is merely one step'. A phrase taken from Voltaire, and one which summed up my frame of mind and helped put a brave face to men who would carry my word far and wide.

I would be doing you a disservice were I not to touch on such setbacks and paint purely a picture of rose cladded gardens, such as those Josephine held so dear at Malmaison. For even now when I close my eyes, all my mistakes parade themselves before me like figures in a nightmare. I wanted too much, I strung the bow too tightly, and I trusted too much in my early good fortune. Maybe there lies the most important message in my notes thus far: success and excess optimism breeds complacency. Stay alert, always.

So, where should I begin? I could fill four volumes on failed actions that proved catastrophic, yet I will touch briefly on the failings which haunt me. At Tilsit, I decided to maintain the Hohenzollern dynasty, which I regret. I crossed the Memel too early—having crossed it in 1812, before I had settled matters in Spain. I regret that in defiance of Carnot's advice, I began my very last campaign too early. At Waterloo, I did not send the guard forward early enough. I did not send Ney to attack Wellington before the arrival of Blucher, nor did I have Murat by my side at the head of the cavalry.

Most of all, when my power was finally broken, I entrusted myself to England, instead of to the Tsar, or, better still, to the United States. This, my final regret, must be my greatest. From the vantage ground of America, I should have been able to guard France against humiliation. The dread of my return would have sufficed. In America, I should have established the centre of a new French fatherland. Within a year, I would have had 60,000 men grouped around me. It would have been the most natural place of refuge—a land of vast expanses where a man can live in freedom.

In Europe, I was too popular, bound up in one way or another, with every nation. As a fugitive, and disguised, I could certainly have escaped to the United States, but both expedients would have been undignified. Joseph even mentioned swapping identities! I put my trust in the approach of danger, thinking that the nation would be forced to turn to me as its saviour, which is why I stayed as long as possible at Malmaison and in Rochefort. The destiny that brought me to St. Helena was the outcome of those feelings.

As a younger man, I would never have made such errors of judgement. For it always took me a clearer mind to take decisive action. Back then, I had a way of arranging things in my mind like a wardrobe. When I wished to put any matter out of my mind, I closed its drawer and opened the belonging to another matter. The contents of the drawers were never mixed, and they never worried me or wearied me. When I retired for the night, I closed all the drawers in my mind, and I fell asleep.

Marcus Aurelius said, 'Every separate action furthers the integrity of your life, and you must be content if every act succeeds as well as it can. No one can stop you achieving this aim.' But no man is an island. We cannot achieve our destiny without ingratiating ourselves upon others. For we must build and maintain relationships with others.

RELATIONSHIPS

'The first method for estimating the

intelligence of a ruler

is to look at the men he has around

him,'

~ Niccolo Machiavelli.

Though I learnt nothing from all of my battles which I did not learn from the first, relationships with women, men and nations are an ongoing battle, and ones that are harder to master. Where should I begin?

Julius Caesar rightly said, 'All men cling naturally to freedom. All men hate servitude.' Your people must feel free, it is their choice to follow, love and respect you. They should be directed without being made aware of it.

In dealing with people, a leader must break his promises when they have put him at a disadvantage and when the reasons for which he made the promises no longer exist. In any case, promises are never something upon which a leader can rely, since men are by nature wretched and deceitful. A leader should be a master of deception. Simply promise everything and deliver nothing. It would not be remiss to say, a leader is a dealer in hope.

And love? Love is naught but a silly infatuation. Depend upon it, and friendship is but a name. I love nobody except my son. I do not even love my brother. Perhaps I do love Joseph, a little, from habit, and because he is my elder, and Duroc, I loved him too; but why? Because his character pleased me. He was stern and resolute, and I believe, the fellow never shed a single tear.

Are you of good nature?

Consider this ... a ruler that garners a reputation for such in the first year of his reign is laughed at in the second. The love that kings inspire should be virile—partly in apprehensive respect, and partly in a thirst for reputation. When a king is said to be a good fellow, his reign is a failure. How can a 'good' fellow—or a good leader, if you will—bear the burdens of royalty, keep malcontents in order, and either silence political passions or enlist them under his own banner?

I must confess, the sight of this Longwood makes me melancholy. Sometimes, I cannot help feeling so negative. Today is such a day. The rain is heavier than ever before. Let's start this conversation once more, re-phrasing my opinion of our fellow man and relationships, forgetting for a moment this wretched house and this damp climate.

For my part, I know very well that I have no true friends, for the shifts of fortune test the reliability of friendship. I am apt to remember the words of Cicero, 'Only those that are to be judged friendships in which the characters have been strengthened and matured by age.' So maybe, I should add Bertrand as my friend in that case, as his sad eyes look disappointed as he dictates these disparate thoughts!

Whilst in power, I had as many pretend friends as I pleased. Leave such sensibilities to women. Men should be firm in heart and purpose, or they should have nothing to do with war and government. However, 'pretend' friendship is vital if one is to grease the wheels of economy. These faux friends of many classes and skills helped build momentum, and I in return, was a good 'friend' to them. In my younger days, I mixed easily with others, took easily to people and listened. Never forget, I was a soldier from the ages of 9 to 27. In such masculine society, friendship was valued above all other things.

I recall my first proclamation to the Army of Italy in 1796. It is astonishing what power words have over men, and it not only set the tone for this campaign, but that of all those to come. Here I was, my paper strength of 43,000 men was down to a little over 30,000, with only 60 cannons, and the men were unpaid. But I did not allow this to deter me, for I had waited too long for such an opportunity. I have always understood that men are more easily governed through their vices than through their virtues. Thus, I promised them loot for our victories. I still remember the words I used:

'Soldiers! You are naked and starving. The government owes you much and can give you nothing. Among these rocks, your patience, your courage, are admirable. But not one ray of glory can shine down on you. I will lead you into the most fertile plain of the earth. Wealthy cities, great provinces, will be in your power; and there await your honour, glory and riches. Soldiers of Italy, will your courage, will your constancy fail?'

This became my soldiers essential *raison d'être*. If they are to unite, to surmount the thousand and one privations they must endure in life and battle, all men must have *raison d'être*, and it must be one they can grasp readily. Never let your men drift. I was always kindly to the men and lavished them with praise. Conversely, to the officers, I was severe.

But even the most generous ideals can go awry once leadership breaks down. I vividly recall writing to Joseph on the evening of 10th August 1792, after the National Guardsmen stormed the Tuileries, massacring the Swiss Guards, and making off with Marie Antoinette's jewels, silver and dresses. Leadership should have come from the king immediately. 'If only Louis XVI had shown himself on horseback, victory would have been his,' I wrote. I learnt a lot that day and was sickened to see respectable-looking women perpetrating outrages on dead Swiss Guards. The anger and hatred on the faces of the mob were not those of generous ideals, the sense of law, justice and fraternity which had launched the Revolution. Times were changing once more.

It is not true that men never change. Men change for the worse as well as for the better. Nor is it true that they are ungrateful.

More often than not, the benefactor rates his favours higher than their worth, and too often he does not allow for changes in circumstance. If few men have the moral force to resist impulses, most men do carry within themselves the germs of virtues as well as of vices, of heroism as well as of cowardice. Such is human nature. Education and circumstances do the rest. And, to echo the thoughts of Epictetus, 'Circumstances don't make the man; they only reveal him to himself.'

Let it be said, men are difficult to judge precisely. Do they realize themselves fully? Had I continued to prosper, most of those who abandoned me would probably never have even considered their treachery. In any case, I was more deserted than betrayed. It was more weakness than treason. They were the regiment of St. Peter—repentance and tears may stand at the gates. Apart from that, who has been more popular, more beloved than I? Whoever left behind more ardent regrets than I? Look at France. Might one not say that, from this cursed rock, I still reign over her?

I contest that all my exertions were directed to illuminate the mass of the nation, instead of brutalizing them by ignorance and superstition.

My force of character has often been praised, yet for my own dear family, I was nothing but a mollycoddle, and they knew it. The first storm over their perseverance, their obstinacy, always carried the day. And from sheer lassitude, they did whatever they liked with me. I made some great errors there. I did not have the luck of Genghis Khan, with his four sons, who knew no emulation save that of serving him well. When I created a King, he at once considered himself Royal by the grace of God; a delusion seized all of them that they were adored, and preferred by the populace more than I. My family never truly understood me. Neither did they understand their debt to me. The respect for their situation, the name and titles they had, came from me and me alone. They have no gratitude. Do they really think my father left them France in his will to share?

My father, though, was a man of intellect and culture. However, he was too fond of his personal pleasure to occupy his time with us children. He would sometimes attempt to excuse our faults. 'Let them be,' said my mother, 'that is not your business, it is for me to look after them.' She did watch over us in truth with a solicitude without equal. Low sentiments and ungenerous feelings were checked and banished. Mother allowed nothing to reach our young spirits that was not fine and elevated. She had the head of a man on the body of a woman. She was both tender and severe. She punished wrongdoing and rewarded good conduct, and she recognised impartially our good and bad actions. Having said that, all that I am and was, I owe to my mother, since she taught me her own principles and encouraged in me the habit of work.

My brothers, like myself, were born in petty circumstances, but they did not force themselves upwards unaided as I did. The man who is to rule France must either be born to greatness, or he must be one of those whose inborn strength enables them to distinguish themselves from the herd, as I have done.

To understand the man, you have to know what was happening in the world when he was twenty. Yet, he will always be moved by two levers only—the levers of fear and self-interest. Your life's work is to find which lever to use on a daily basis.

It is a truth that man is difficult to know. Furthermore, if we are not to deceive ourselves, we must judge him by his actions of the moment, and for the moment only. As men all have their virtues, their vices, their heroism, and their perverseness, they also possess and exercise all that is good, and all that is bad in this world. I recall the dawn after the battle of Borodino, officers stumbled across a prostate body. Hearing a cry of pain, I ordered whoever it was to be placed on a stretcher. 'It's only a Russian', murmured an aide, whereupon I snapped back, 'After victory there are no enemies, only men.'

Men need to share, or believe they are sharing, the secrets of whomever commands them. This is how one creates the little group of the faithful around oneself.

The Legion of Honour drew considerable criticism from those who considered it inappropriate to the principles of liberty and equality won by blood spilled in the revolution. Some even regarded the award as a return step toward monarchy, because of its proclaimed elitism and monarchy's penchant for colourful titles and elaborated crosses and ribbons. My response always echoed these words ... men are led by toys. I don't think that the French particularly love liberty and equality. The French are not at all charged by ten years of revolution. They are what the Gauls were—fierce and fickle. They have one feeling, however and one we must nourish. They must have distinctions.

A General's most important talent is to

know the mind of the soldier and gain his confidence, and in both respects, the French soldier is more difficult to lead than another. He is not a machine that must be made to move, he is a reasonable being who needs leadership.

And finally, always look a man in the eye, the effect you have on others is the most valuable currency you have. My first impression of Lowe, my goaler, was that he failed to look me in the eye. One must not pass hasty judgement, but I firmly hoped his character was different from his looks. He reminds me of a Sicilian policeman.

Look your men in the eye. Show them you have the knowledge and integrity to lead them to the darkest corners of the Universe.

KNOWLEDGE

'One who thoughtfully ponders the

centuries, surveys the whole in the clear

light of the spirit;

All that is petty has vanished from sight;

Oceans and continents alone are of

account'

~ Goethe.

Show me a family of readers, and I will show you the people who move the world. For, you must crave knowledge as a woman craves compliments.

As a penniless cadet, I would often look at the books in the bookstores with the sin of envy. I coveted them for a long time before my purse allowed me to buy. Such were the joys and seductions of my youth. And then, when I had finally saved two ècus of six livres, I would hurry like a happy child to the bookstore.

With libraries, reading is as free as breathing, but when a man has read all the books in the lending library, he must spare a little money now and again to buy a new book.

I joined my regiment in Valence, a sub-lieutenant, compelled by poverty to walk a great part of the way, I hasten to add. I lodged in a café, and the clicking of the billiard balls in the adjoining room was tiresome. Of course, a young man should learn to dance and taste the pleasure of lively society. My pride held me back in an attempt to hide my poverty. Instead of cavorting in such a way, I read, absorbed and allowed my imagination to roam the world. The reading of history soon made me feel as though I was capable of achieving as much as the men who are placed in the highest ranks of our annals. I only focused on books which I hoped to be of use to me one day. I still have copy-books on the following titles: Artillery, its principles and history; the art of siege; Plato's Republic; the constitution of the Persian, the Athenian, the Spartan State; the history of England; the campaigns of Frederick the Great; French finances; the Tartars and the Turks, their manners and customs, and the topography of their countries; the history of Egypt and the history of Carthage; descriptions of India; English accounts of contemporary France; Mirabeau, Buffon and Machiavelli; the history and the constitution of Switzerland; the history and constitution of China, India, the Inca State; the history of the nobility and the story of patrician misdeed. I also retain books on astronomy, geology and meteorology; the laws of the growth of population; statistics of mortality.

Tactics, evolutions, the science of the engineer and the artillerist can be learned from books, almost like geometry, but the knowledge of the heroic facts of war can only be acquired by study of the history of wars, the battles of great captains, and by experience too, I hasten to add.

Moreover, I did not simply flutter the pages but was an attentive reader and took copious notes, most of which I still have, although many are almost illegible. In fact, the final entry in my copybooks reads, 'St. Helena, a small island in the Atlantic Ocean. English colony.' Ah, the irony!

When accepting membership to the National Institute of Sciences and Arts, in 1797, I distilled my greatest accolade to acquiring knowledge, and one I still believe should drive man. It is thus:

'True conquests, the only ones which leave no regrets, are those made over ignorance. The most honourable and useful occupation for nations is to contribute to the extension of human knowledge. The true power of the French Republic should consist henceforth in allowing no single new idea to escape its embrace.'

Remember, to be a genius, one need only study hard enough to be able to tell the people what they already think. This, I feel, is why my Civil Code will survive for centuries. Because of its simplicity, it has already done more good in France than the sum total of all the laws that preceded it. And also, my schools will prepare unknown generations. All my laws were liberal, even those concerning conscription and the state prisons: the people were never my enemies, in any country.

To lead an army, one must ceaselessly attend to it, be ahead of the news, provide for everything. This was always my duty. And, as I stood on the bridge of L'Orient, gazing into the glimmering horizon of the Mediterranean, I believed I had not only tended to my army's needs, but also the vast group of geographers, architects, civil engineers, economists, journalists, balloonists, scientists, professors, painters and naturists, in preparation of the invasion of Egypt. It was a venture on a scale never seen before.

I would follow in the footsteps of Alexander and Caesar. Alexander the Great said, 'Without knowledge, skill cannot be focused. Without skill, strength cannot be brought to bear, and without strength, knowledge may not be applied.' It was my quest to gain the knowledge for France and then apply our strength. And this, I felt, I achieved. I had even carried out surveys to trace a water route along the Suez with my chief engineer General Cafferelli. Remember too, it was France who discovered the Rosetta Stone; the black basalt slab was inscribed with ancient writing and found near the town of Rosetta, east of Alexandria. The irregularly shaped stone contained fragments of passages written in three different scripts: Greek, Egyptian hieroglyphics and Egyptian demotic. The British stole it from us in 1801, it was not their discovery! My departure from Egypt was hurried, as my presence in Paris was needed, albeit for my benefit. Destiny called.

I will finish today's notes by saying that the day-to-day knowledge of your assets and your men's performances is essential. You must make it your first duty of the day to read the muster rolls of your armies. I gain more pleasure from this kind of reading than a young girl acquires from reading a novel. This is your way of knowing the exact positions and composition of each unit in your army.

As leader, it is your responsibility to be constantly aware of how your men are reacting to their needs. For the primal thirst of an army that lacks everything will always be quenched, and let it also be said, a soldier who lacks bread is driven to excess of lust and violence which makes one blush for humanity.

LUST

'A common lust, an absurd passion,

Swayed the hardened devil foolishly,'

~ Goethe

Faust: Act V Scene VI:

The Great Outer Court of the Palace

Bertrand has titled this lesson **LUST**, and felt you deserving of a more intimate conversation. As commander of all, lust will appear daily. Like all desires, this one intrigues and gives false hope.

Lust of women sways the hardened devil foolishly, as Goethe so famously stated. I agree, but for me today, bah, if you don't think of women, you don't need them. But my sad youthful days left deep scars. I would write and dream. My notebooks reveal a man I have all but forgotten. Filled with romantic melancholy, I was a child of the ages, nourished on Goethe's Werther. I saw myself as Rousseau's Virtuous Man. That is, virtue in the Latin sense of the word. I believed, men in Corsica were ruled by love of their fatherland, as they had been in Roman and Spartan times. Whereas the French people were, and are, entirely absorbed in eroticism. From the austere life we lived at Casa Buonaparte, the harsh countryside of Corsica, and it's poor and frugal society, so close to Rousseau's ideals were totally opposed to life in corrupt, luxury loving France. In France, I was all alone in the midst of men. What I was to do in this world, vexed me continuously.

I wrote my first novel, Clisson & Eugenie, in my early twenties. It was a time when young men romanticized the hero's death and talked of love and lust. Uncannily, my life played out in a similar manner to the books I wrote and read.

I must confess, I would often visit the Parisian fleshpots of the Palais Royal, where the honest and prudent man—who involves himself only in his own affairs—has the freedom to live as he wishes. The more expensive whores had their rooms on the mezzanine of the arcades, from whose half-moon windows they could lean out and call to passers-by or adopt suggestive poses in the embrasures. The better-known ones sent runners circulating in the crowds below to hand out leaflets describing their specialities and prices. Lesser prostitutes lurked in the palace gardens, and this is where I headed. I wrote to Joseph at the time that, the memory of the Terror is no more than a nightmare here. Everyone appears determined to make up for what they have suffered. Determined also, not to miss a single pleasure of the present.

Desire reawakens the enjoyment of being alive. And if one is to impose oneself on this world, then one must first conquer and possess a woman. As a young man of twenty-six, I recall that in Paris women were everywhere. In the theatres, out driving, in the libraries. In the scholar's study, you see great belles. Here alone of all the places on earth, they deserve to govern. Plus, the men are mad about them, think of nothing else and live only by and for them. A woman needed but six-months in Paris to know what is her due and the extent of her empire.

In time, I was gradually introduced to the Salons of the most beautiful and powerful women of Paris, by my then mentor, for want of a better word, Paul Barras. At first, I was uncomfortable. During these visits, I made the acquaintance of my incomparable Josephine, and my life would never be the same.

I awake full of you, your face, our intoxicating evening, have excited all my senses ... I take from your lips, from your heart a scalding flame ... Mio dolce amore, a million kisses, but give none to me for they set my blood on fire.

This is one of many passionate notes I have copies of, which Bertrand has found. I will not bore you with others. We were married in a Paris registry office in March 1796. I upped my age to 28, and she reduced hers to 29. I chose Josephine for no other reason than desire. It would be fair judgement to say that I lusted day and night for her, and she, less so. As always, she needed money and stability for her two young children. But I was in love and nothing else mattered. Then, after our brief time in Paris together, I was off to battle. The Italian campaign beckoned, and my star would not falter. It is true, she cuckolded me. Maybe it was retribution that the tables turned. I took mistress after mistress, starting as early as the Egyptian campaign, and often flaunting my indiscretions openly in front of her as time went by. Since I had several sons from such liaisons, I knew for certain it was she who was barren, and I desperately needed a son to continue the Empire. Divorce was inevitable.

Now, I am older and wiser and wish you to profit from my counsel. Women, I can assure you, belong to the highest bidder. Power is what they like. It is the greatest of aphrodisiacs. They are fascinated by it. As for me, I took them and forgot them. They are mere machines for making children.

I have always hated manipulative scheming women. I am accustomed to and enthralled by ones who are gentle, sweet and captivating. For when they are bad, they are worse than men, and more ready to commit crime. When degraded, they fall lower than men. Witness the *tricoteuses de Paris* during the Revolution.

A woman laughing is a woman conquered, yet I still also like to tease. A few weeks ago, I riled Mme Montholon and Mme Bertrand, as I often do simply to engender a response. I stated matter-of-factly that, for every woman who inspires us to do good things, there are hundreds who bring us folly. Really, we Westerners do not understand women at all. We have spoiled everything by treating them far too well. It was utterly wrong to lift women up almost to our own level. The Orientals managed these things much better.

They maintain that woman is man's property; and in every truth, nature makes woman to be the slave of man. Let the Madame's believe what they wish to believe, I received a reaction to starve off my boredom!

Remember young commander, I am no saint or capuchin. Though I have remarked more than once that sexual love was harmful, both to society and to the individual happiness of men, I would be a fool if I did not allow a man to be a man. We all have our rutting seasons, as the noises made at Longwood by fornicating servants, soldiers and sailors can attest to. More annoyance than this was caused by de Montholon when he complained to Lowe about the noises and that whores had been brought in. In response, Lowe immediately placed more sentries on duty. Idiots, the both of them. We should have dealt with it ourselves. I feel de Montholon is in need of a young lady too, especially now his Albine is set to leave for Paris, with my baby girl!

ENERGY

'Why do you fear your last day? It contributes no more to your death than each of the others. The last step does not cause the fatigue but reveals it. All day's travel towards death, the last one reaches it,'

~ Michael De Montaigne.

Energy is the final lesson I feel obliged to share with you, my young commander. This is poignant—as my strength and energy ebbs from my grasp—that I attempt to discuss it with enthusiasm. Energy cannot be taught, but without it, a man cannot know himself, create power, take constant action, build relationships or gain knowledge. Energy comes disguised as discipline, work and desire.

For me, Shakespeare was no Racine or Corneille. I find his plays are pitiful, but I admit, as I age, I relate to these words from his great work, Julius Caesar:

'There is a tide in the affairs of men
Which, taken at the flood, leads on to
fortune;
Omitted, all the voyage of their life
Is bound in shallows and in miseries.
On such a full sea are we now afloat;
And we must take the current when it serves,
Or lose our ventures.'

Admittedly, there is but one step from triumph to downfall. I have seen, in the most significant of circumstances, that some little thing often decides great events. And the further Bertrand delves into my correspondences and copies of written letters in my portfolio, the more I understand the little things which conspired to my destruction; I ignored warning signs and persisted, after all, I was the man of Austerlitz. As Ovid stated, 'The cause is hidden. The effect is visible to all.'

As 1813 approached, I felt my star

setting. Everything in this world must come to an end—wit, sentiment, the sun itself. I had believed my powers would decline eventually and I would grow fat at forty, although I always rode twenty or twenty-five leagues a day on horseback.

Uneasiness stimulates zeal was always a guiding principle for me. As 1811 arrived, I returned to many old habits. Although I lunched alone and stayed in my office longer, I seemed to be working slower and capriciously. In hindsight, I spent far too much time on trivialities, such as court etiquette and dress, all the time neglecting to take command of my army in Spain once more. Joseph was King of Spain, and would take greater control, since I had paved the way with 200,000 men after his earlier debacles. After all, a country full of monks should not have been hard to subdue. Yet, I knew Spain was an unending haemorrhage. The price of bread rose by one hundred percent in France; a warning I would never have neglected when younger. Financial crises loomed and the Continental System was so flawed, it would never bring Britain to its knees. The Tsar, having opened his ports to 'neutral' shipping, created yet another gap, only adding to our deteriorating relationship. The Russians, I decided, would have to learn the lesson for trading with our enemies. I proceeded to mobilize the greatest army in history. Over 675,000 men would march on Moscow. Though intended to be a show of power, too much escalated too soon. And, though advised to finish the Spanish campaign first, I believed it was in my power to advance north simultaneously and win on both fronts.

This was my proclamation to the Grand Army:

'Soldiers! The second Polish war has begun; the first ended at Friedland and Tilsit. At Tilsit, Russia pledged an eternal alliance with France, and war on England! Today her oath is broken. She refuses all explanations of her strange conduct unless the French eagles recross the Rhine. Fate draws Russia on. Her destiny must be accomplished! Does she then think us degenerate? Are we no longer the soldiers of Austerlitz? She places us between dishonour and war. Can our choice be in doubt? Forward, then, across the Niemen, and let us carry the war to her own soil!

Energetically, I crossed the Niemen first and galloped ahead of my Guard. But I have to admit, I tumbled from my horse as a hare crossed my path, many called it an omen to turn back, but in the words of Julius Caesar, when he crossed the Rubicon, *the die had been cast,* there was no turning back.

'We shan't repeat Charles XII's mistake,' I stated as we crossed the barren landscape of Russia, and then added something along the lines of, 'When the army has rested, while the weather is still temperate, we shall return via Smolensk to winter in Lithuania and Poland.' Which, at the time, I firmly believed. Yet, I was drawn deeper and deeper into the Russian heartlands. After the battle of Borodino, we continued to advance. There was no further resistance, and we reached the outskirts of Moscow. I recall it was a bright sunny afternoon, 13th September 1812, almost three months after crossing the Niemen. The sun reflected on all the domes, spires and gilded palaces. It was a sight to behold, magical. At this magnificent sight troubles, dangers, fatigues, privations were forgotten.

'There it is at last. And high time,' I stated.

I believed we would have good winter quarters and play the Tsar at his own games. For what could go wrong?

We entered the city on the 15th September.

People have said I stayed too long in Moscow, but the weather was beautiful, and I was waiting for peace. A great political drama!

In my defence, who could have foreseen the Russians burning their own great city too?

During our retreat, we were defeated by mother nature, as the excessive and premature severity of the winter bore down our army in a frightful calamity. In the space of a few nights, all was changed. France suffered great losses. If, in such circumstances, I could have allowed myself to think of anything but the interests, the glory, and the future of my people, my spirit and energies would have been broken.

Once the remnants of my defeated army were safe in Poland, I hastened back to Paris with faithful Caulincourt, to raise another army and put to rest my demise. It was an arduous journey, but my energy sustained me, though this was the beginning of the end for me.

Past evils are without remedy and despite the losses in Russia, I fielded a new army of formidable size, yet one composed increasingly of younger conscripts. I was forced to call up those due for service some years ahead of their due time. In February 1813, Prussia joined forces with Russia and allied states began to drift from my grasp. This became the signal for an upsurge in German nationalism and resulted in the War of Liberation. The battlefields beckoned. It was time to make war. We would hurl these

Tartars back into that frightful clime whence they must never more depart. Let them remain in their frozen steppes, the abode of slavery, of barbarism, and of corruption, where man is reduced to the level of the brute!

My army tasted success once again. The young guard fought with energy and zeal. With seventy-thousand men, we repulsed a hundred and fifty-thousand foe for Dresden. Nothing could equal the courage, the good-will, the devotion that all these young soldiers showed me. They were full of enthusiasm.

But what the history books may foretell is, I had lounged after the battle of Dresden and spent the day in a curious apathy before my campfire. It will be true, I was unwell. In war good health is indispensable. Yet also, I found this new 'game of chess' becoming confused, as my political vision became impaired along with the strategist within me. I am apt to remember the words of Plato, 'One man cannot practice many arts with success.' But I needed the Austrians upon my side.

In quick succession, I lost both Bessières and my great friend Duroc, who only moments before, had been at my side before a cannonball tore open the lower part of his body. I was devastated.

Alas, war rekindled in northern Europe proved a favourable opportunity for the English to act in the Peninsula. War can be conducted only with energy, decision, and constant resolution. There must be no experimenting, no hesitation. Maintain strict discipline, and when you go into action, show confidence in your men. But time was running away from me. 15,000 of my men were without muskets!

Had the enemy learnt my lessons?

Bertrand has found several old bulletins. In 1805 are the words:

'It rains hard, but that does not stop the march of the Grand army.'

Then again in 1806, I boasted:

'While people are deliberating, the French army is marching.'

Now, during this critical time, the enemy marched and I laboured in apathy!

Metternich, the Austrian envoy, brought forth a tardy mediation that looked hostile. I urged Caulaincourt to try for direct negotiations. I wanted peace, a solid peace, but on honourable terms. The Austrians could not remain neutral any longer. 'We must be for you, or against you,' Metternich stated. And the day after a six-week truce, the

Austrians declared war on France.

Although exhausted, I could not abase neither the nation nor myself by accepting such shameful terms. I was determined to fight on, and I made the following declaration:

'For every Frenchman with a heart, the moment has come to conquer or perish!'

With fewer than 80,000 men I faced 300,000 Russians, Prussians and Austrians on the Rhine, and 100,000 British, Spanish and Portuguese coming over the Pyrenees. I am fond of saying, against greatly superior forces it is possible to win a battle, but hardly a war, and this was the position forced upon me. Abdication was inevitable, and in return for such agitation and heartache, I was rewarded with Elba as my principality!

My time in Elba, as you know, was short-lived. I kept myself busy and absorbed myself in restructuring the island. But it would never satisfy my desires. My destiny laid unfulfilled, my mother agreed too, and told me it would be far more honourable to die with a sword in one's hand. I planned my escape thoroughly and returned to Paris without a single shot fired. My old energies surged once more, and I worked night and day to make France great again. But it was to no avail, momentum had been lost long ago. The great nation had tired of war and of losing its sons. With our energies and resources depleted and the losses of the battle of Waterloo, it was merely a matter of time before I finally abdicated again. This time, my enemies ensured my energy and passion would no longer threaten their arrogance and egotistical supremacy.

Reputation is the one thing that outlives us. Men die, women die, all things must die, but reputation lives on. It echoes through the theatres, the history books and music we listen to in rapt attention. All men crave reputation, and I am as guilty as the next. So, remember to your dying days, everything passes swiftly apart from the opinion we leave imprinted on history. This, my young commander, I have achieved. My only remaining wish is to have instilled in you a life-long passion to follow your star of destiny and to **SPARKLE** like no other in creation.

Adieu *mon Commandant, mon Roi, mon beau fils,*

N.

HISTORICAL NOTES

Barras, Paul (1755-1829). One of the most important political figures of the later Revolutionary period. Barras became friendly toward Napoleon, whom he first encountered in Toulon. As a Director, his notorious immorality and avarice did much to undermine the reputation of that body, thus facilitating the coup of Brumaire, which brought Napoleon to power. His political career ended with the fall of the Directory, whereupon he retired to enjoy his dubiously accumulated wealth. Josephine was one of his mistresses prior to her marriage to Napoleon. Many say Barras became bored with Josephine and pre-arranged Napoleon's first few encounters with her to make way for a younger mistress.

Bertrand, General Henri-Gratien (1733-1844). Originally an engineer, he was one of the most loyal of Napoleon's subordinates, serving as his aide, as governor-general of Illyria (1811-12), and from January 1813 as commander of the corps of observation of Italy. He accompanied Napoleon to both Elba and St. Helena, and escorted Napoleon's body on its repatriation to France in 1840. Bertrand's half-English wife, Fanny, also went with her husband to St. Helena, though she had pleaded with Napoleon not to take him. Though Napoleon dictated many of his thoughts to his faithful followers and hoped they would profit when they returned to France, I felt it was only fitting for *Napoleon: Way of the Conqueror*, to be composed by General Bertrand.

Duc d'Enghien, Louis-Antoine-de Bourbon-Condè (1772-1804). A French Royalist who was the subject of one of the actions for which Napoleon was most criticised. Napoleon believed that Enghien was implicated in Royalist plots, which in fact was not the case. Napoleon ordered that he be seized by a raid into neutral territory (Ettenheim in Baden) in March 1804. He was summarily tried and shot in the moat of Vincennes Castle. Josephine was appalled and pleaded with Napoleon not to go through with it. Years later he still said he would do it again, as he disbelieved the evidence.

Longwood, St. Helena. Was the main residence for Napoleon and where he passed away. Longwood was originally a farm belonging to the East India Company and was afterwards given as a country residence to the Deputy-Governor. The Duke of Wellington stayed there also, many years before on his return from service in India. It was converted for the use of Napoleon in 1815. The British government eventually recognized its inadequacy as a home for the former Emperor and his entourage and, by the time of his death, had built a new house for him nearby, which he never occupied. In February 1818, **Governor Sir Hudson Lowe** proposed to **Lord Bathurst** to move Napoleon to Rosemary Hall, a house that became available and was located in a more hospitable part of the island, sheltered from the winds and shaded, as Napoleon had preferred. But the revelations of **General Gourgaud** in London brought Lord Bathurst to the opinion that it was safer to keep Napoleon at Longwood, where an escape was harder to undertake. The building of the new house only began in October 1818, three years after Napoleon's arrival on the island. Napoleon spent his first two-months at The Briars, whilst Longwood was being prepared.

Lowe, General Sir Hudson (1769 - 1844). A British expert on Mediterranean warfare (he commanded the Corsican Rangers), Lowe was rejected by Wellington for a position on his staff in 1815, but become Napoleon's 'gaoler' as governor of St Helena. He was condemned by Napoleon and his entourage for his unsympathetic behaviour toward them, although he met Napoleon only four times during the entire period of his confinement. Lowe was damned if he did and damned if he didn't, it was a no-win situation for him and he was simply carrying out orders by those who paid him. But the pettiness displayed by him for such things as, not addressing Napoleon in the right form and charging Napoleon for books to study and record his memoirs, did little to enamour him to the small court held by Napoleon; which they subsequently displayed in the literature they wrote when they returned to France and published their accounts of the Emperor's time on St Helena.

Montholon, Charles-Tristan, comte de (1783 – 1853). A staff officer of no great distinction, he fell out of favour with Napoleon and accused of embezzlement in 1814. Montholon volunteered to accompany Napoleon to St Helena, taking with him his wife Albine. Napoleon did not doubt Montholon's loyalty, but it had been suggested many years before he may have been implicated in Royalist plots to murder him. Montholon wrote successful books about Napoleon's time on St Helena. His wife, Albine, was Napoleon's last mistress, and it was said she had a daughter by him whom she named Joséphine-Napoléone; who died as an infant in Paris. An interesting fact concerning Montholon is that he also shared the captivity of Napoleon III at Ham Prison, from 1840 to 1846 – the same length of time he had shared with his uncle in St Helena.

CHRONOLOGY OF EVENTS

1768

Corsica reunited with France

1769

15 August: Napoleon, second son of
Carlo Bonaparte and Letizia Ramolino,
born in Ajaccio, Corsica.

1774

10 May: Louis XVI ascends throne of
France.

1779

Napoleon admitted to the Ecole
Militaire in Brienne.

1784

Napoleon chosen for the Ecole
Militaire in Paris.

1785

Death of Carlos Bonaparte.

Napoleon receives his first posting to Valence, as a second-lieutenant in a regiment of artillery.

1789

Start of the French Revolution.

5 May: Estates-General assembles at Versailles.

14 July: Fall of the Bastille.

26 August: Declaration of the Rights of Man.

September: Napoleon returns to Corsica on leave.

1790

Napoleon politically active in Corsica.

1791

January: Napoleon joins the Jacobins.

February: He re-joins his regiment.

20 June: Flight of the French royal family to Varennes.

October: Napoleon returns to Corsica.

1792

10 August: Napoleon witnesses the storming of the Tuileries.

1793

21 January: Louis XVI guillotined.

11 June: The Bonaparte family takes refuge in mainland France.

September-December: Napoleon distinguishes himself at the siege of Toulon.

22 December: Napoleon is appointed general of brigade by Robespierre.

1794

February: Napoleon appointed commander of artillery in the Army of Italy.

27 July: The fall of Robespierre.

8 August: Napoleon arrested but released through the intervention of his

patron Saliceti.

1795

5 October: Napoleon turns his cannon on insurgents besieging the National Convention.

1796

8 March: Napoleon marries Josephine.

11 March: Napoleon appointed Commander-in-Chief of the Army of Italy.

1797

4 September: Coup d'état of 18 Fructidor.

1798

19 May: The French army set sail from Toulon to invade Egypt.

1 August: Nelson destroys French fleet at the Battle of the Nile.

1799

22 August: Napoleon sets sail back to France, leaving General Jean-Baptiste Kléber in charge of the the French Army.

9 November: Napoleon's coup d'état of 18 Brumaire establishes the Consulate.

1800

19 February: Napoleon moves into the Tuileries.

May: The second Italian campaign begins.

14 June: Austrians defeated at the Battle of Marengo.

1802

25 March: Treaty of Amiens signed with Great Britain.

2 August: Napoleon made Consul for life.

1803

18 May: British break the Treaty of Amiens and declares war on France. Napoleon plans to invade Britain.

1804

20-21 March: Kidnap and execution of the Duc d'Enghien.

18 May: The Senate confers upon Napoleon the title of Emperor.

2 December: Napoleon's coronation at Notre Dame.

1807

7 July: Peace of Tilsit with Tsar Alexander.

1808

March: The French occupy Spain. Joseph Bonaparte placed on throne.

1809

15 December: Napoleon divorces

Josephine.

1810

22 April: Napoleon marries the Archduchess Marie-Louise of Austria.

1811

20 March: Birth of Napoleon's son, who is given the title of King of Rome.

1812

May: Napoleon invades Russia.

1813

Coalition formed between Russia, Prussia, Great Britain, Sweden and Austria.

1814

January – March: Allied forces invade France and march into Paris.

11 April: Napoleon abdicates and departs for Elba.

29 May: Josephine dies.

1815

26 February: Napoleon escapes from Elba.

20 March: Napoleon arrives in Paris.

18 June: The French army defeated at Waterloo.

22 June: Napoleon abdicates for the second time.

15 July: Napoleon surrenders to the British and boards the Bellerophan. Also known as The Billy Ruffian. He is taken to Torbay and then Plymouth.

7 August: Napoleon boards the Northumberland for Exile on St. Helena.

1821

5 May: Napoleon dies on St. Helena at the age of 52.

BIBLIOGRAPHY

Asprey, Robert, *The Rise and Fall of Napoleon Bonaparte, Vol 1 2000*

Asprey, Robert, *The Rise and Fall of Napoleon Bonaparte, Vol 2 2001*

Bruce, Evangeline, *Napoleon & Josephine 1995*

Cleare, C.R, *Napoleon 1927*

Cronin, Vincent, *Napoleon 1971*

Dwyer, Philip, *Napoleon – The Path to Power 1769-1799 2008*

Emerson, Ralph Waldo, *Essays and Representative Men, Vol 1 1904*

Gallo, Max, *Napoleon – The Song of Departure 2004*

Gallo, Max, Napoleon – The Sun of Austerlitz 2004

Gallo, Max, *Napoleon – The Emperor of Kings 2004*

Gallo, Max, *Napoleon – The Immortal of St. Helena 2005*

Haythornthwaite, Philip & Johnstone,R,M, *In The Words Of Napoleon 2002*

Hibbert, Christopher, *Napoleon - His Wives and Women 2002*

Horne, Alistair, *How Far From Austerlitz? Napoleon 1805-1815 1996*

Johnson, Paul, *Napoleon 2003*

Ludwig, Emil, *Napoleon 1927*

McNair Wilson, R, *Napoleon The Man 1927*

O'Connor Morris, William, *Napoleon Warrior and Ruler 1907*

Roberts, Andrew, *Napoleon the Great 2014*

Thompson, J.M, *Letters of Napoleon 1934*

Zamoyski, Adam, *Napoleon – The Man Behind the Myth 2018*

FREE BONUS GIFT

As a special thank you for your support and making it this far please download my Code of the Conqueror – The Journey and feel free to share it with the world:)

Thanks for being here😊

[Click Here To Download](#)

[Code of the Conqueror -The Journey](#)

Or use the link below in your browser

https://dl.bookfunnel.com/vpow o1dk3w

About Mark Weeks

Mark Weeks is a bestselling Amazon author who has a passion for inspiring and teaching others to take greater control of their lives.

Mark's mission is to empower people through strategies, tools and his fictional novels to help them design a life they want to live and not have to live.

Having spent his life thus far, as a builder, entrepreneur, investor, writer and online publisher he refuses to be pigeon-holed, and believes to live a life on your terms, you too should create multiple income streams to create freedom and a life without limits.

And in light of the pandemic, it's even more important to reflect and act upon how we approach both our working lives and social lives.

Mark lives in Leeds, Kent with his childhood sweetheart and best friend, Kim and continues to create multiple income streams; including many more novels and self-help courses.

Contact Mark via email on mark@urconqueror.co.uk or via his facebook page

To find out more about Mark's self-leadership work visit urconqueror.co.uk or for publishing and creating multiple income streams visit Azuni.World
If that's not up your street then Visit Mark's Amazon page

Other books by Mark …
Code of the Conqueror – The Journey
Introduces you to the first of Mark's unique 12 keys to an enlightened life. Through the teachings of the enigmatic Yelu Bao-Zhi you will grasp the concept we should not grasp after our desires. As in every area of life – balance is the key! Come and join Zhi as he teaches hapless entrepreneur Alex the art of desire.

<u>Timeless Wisdom</u> 701 Inspirational Quotes to Conquer Life

We all need to stay motivated and as much as we may try by ourselves, we need a 'pick me-up' every now and again. Within these 701 quotes you will find the motivation to re-new, re-shape and invigorate your life.

<u>Conquerors: Military History Quotes 450 BC-1788 AD</u>

'The man, whom you should admire and imitate is the one who finds it a joy to live and in spite of that is not reluctant to die.' ~ Seneca - Letters from a Stoic The 155 quotes within part one of Conquerors, distils the knowledge and wisdom from history's warriors, kings and philosophers, revealing that inner sanctum where life hangs by a single thread.

<u>Mum Ultrapreneur</u>

Published over 13 years ago and co-written with Mark's great friend Susan Odev, Mum Ultrapreneur is even more relevant in today's society than it was in 2007. That's the trouble when you're ahead of the game – people forget about you – te he 😊 😊

mum
ultrapreneur
"Filled to breaking with
the insights of over thirty
incredible business mums"
Saira Khan Director of Miamoo,
author of 'PUSH for Success' and
Star of TV's The Apprentice
discover the 8 essential secrets
to starting, running and building a
successful mum-based business
susan ödev and mark weeks

CODE
OF THE
CONQUEROR
THE JOURNEY
DESIRE IS INEVITABLE. SURRENDER IS OPTIONAL.
THE ART OF SELF-MASTERY FOR A 21st CENTURY CONQUEROR
MARK WEEKS

FREE BONUS GIFT

As a special thank you for your

support and making it this far

please download this free book

and share it with the world:)

Thanks for being here

Click Here To Download

Code of the Conqueror -The

Journey

Or use the link below in your

browser

https://dl.bookfunnel.com/vpow

o1dk3w

The End – until we meet again 😊

If you would like to learn more about Code of the Conqueror – Art of Manfulness please email me at mark@urconqueror.co.uk

Keep a look out for my Age of Heroes novel in December 2021 too, please.

www.ingramcontent.com/pod-product-compliance
Lightning Source LLC
Chambersburg PA
CBHW031414250726
48656CB00002B/674